THE LITTLE BOOK
OF NEW YORK

THE LITTLE BOOK OF NEW YORK

Christine Barrely

CHÊNE

SKYLINE OF DOWNTOWN NEW YORK CITY AS SEEN FROM HUDSON RIVER

37

3A-H1298

CONTENTS

SKYLINE OF DOWNTOWN NEW YORK CITY AS SEEN FROM BROOKLYN AT NIGHT

5A-H652

HISTORY OF A CITY

It's the city of all superlatives- a city that gladly accepts the title of Capital of the World. And really, what other city could possibly dispute the title? It's an odd city, tucked between land and sea, the islands and the continent, and is the fruit of a rushed history. Barely four centuries have gone by since that day in 1626 when the Native Americans agreed to sell their island to Peter Minuit, a Dutch colonist. The new small colony took on the name of New Amsterdam, in honor of his native land. A few farms and a village later, and the island of Manhattan had begun its urban conversion. In 1664, the English took over the site and changed the name to New York, in honor of the Duke of York. Nothing went as they planned though, with English dominance increasingly contested, leading to the declaration of independence in 1776.

Galloping growth

The city kept its name, but launched into a frenzy of growth. Real estate promoters and financiers speculated and embarked on increasingly ambitious projects. The city, which started at the southern tip of the island, quickly spread past its initial limits and extended towards the north. In 1807, an urbanization committee decided to establish a precise plan for all future developments. Its efforts led to the famous Randel Plan of 1811, which created a strict grid pattern making streets and avenues meet at right angles. The New York City street map was born. Over the following decades, developing construction progressively filled up the layout. Manors and small buildings welcomed the incredible melting pot that the city had become. Waves of migrations, and the successes and failures of major colonial families fed the population growth that never stopped. In 1810 there were 120,000 residents, and by 1900 that number had grown to 3.4 million before doubling to 7 million in 1930 and an approximate 8.4 million people today. The city of New York has grown and changed constantly over the course of catastrophes, fires, epidemics, economic crises, and terrorist attacks, but like the phoenix from the ashes, it is always reborn stronger, more beautiful, and more intense.

Of wood and brick, of iron or steel

As with all first settlements in the United States, wood was the first construction material used by colonial settlers. Quickly though, the rich landowners invested in the local rock that could be quarried or in brick that both lent themselves brilliantly to the architectural style that had been imported from England. To demonstrate their success and surprise Old Europe that served as inspiration, the New York architects of the 19th century rivaled one another in audacity, confidently mixing together a variety of styles, with little regard to chronology or subtlety. The initial classical inspiration quickly gave way to neo-roman fantasy, but also neo-gothic, neo-Renaissance and Byzantine architectural feats. And, with lots of land increasing in both rarity and price, the architects looked skywards: ten, fifteen, fifty stories high! At the end of the 19th century, New York entered into the era of skyscrapers. Experts still argue today who exactly built the first such tower: Chicago or New York? The architects of the Chicago school are certainly the most internationally renown, but the large-scale multiplication of such buildings is instantly recognized as a characteristic of New York at the start of the 20th century. The Manhattan Life Insurance Building (1894), the Park Row Building (1899), the Metropolitan Life Insurance Tower (1909) and the Woolworth Building (1913) all beat the world record for tallest building. To reconcile esthetics and business profit, the most innovative and practical methods were sought out. The legendary method of cast iron allowed for tall buildings punctuate with numerous windows and decorated with a plethora of sculptures, friezes, and trimmings of all kinds.

The famous Flatiron Building, inaugurated in 1902, is most emblematic of this style and technique. Soon though, steel bones and other metalwork surpassed iron and brick. In New York, business is business and profit comes first, so builders were often quick to demolish older structures in order to replace them with grander, taller, more profitable towers. The first Waldorf Astoria hotel, for example, was demolished in order for the Empire State Building to be built.

MIDTOWN SKYLINE SHOWING CHRYSLER BUILDING AND RADIO CITY, NEW YORK

14815

A Catalogue of styles

Absolute eclecticism reigned over New York. It was in the form of neo-antique temples, as in the case of the New York Stock Exchange and Federal Hall, or neo-gothic structures like the Woolworth Building. New York also showed itself to be quite fond of a style that came to be nicknamed "Beaux-Arts", in reference to the art school in Paris where many American architects learned their craft. This style gave way to such landmarks as the New York Public Library and Grand Central Terminal. At times, it is difficult to identify exactly which style a building belongs to, when it is more an assembly of heritages surpassing classic architectural canon. The Municipal Building is an example of such chimeras. In reality, New York spent many years searching for its own identity. One style in particular, which flourished in the 1920's, finally gave the city its dignified calling card: the Art-Deco movement. Once again, the inspiration came from Europe, with the French, Viennese, and German schools of architecture, but New York shone by elaborating on the style on a grand scale that the Old Continent had only developed on a small one. The Chrysler building, a sparkling jewel with its dramatic metallic scales is undoubtedly its most flamboyant manifestation. But it wasn't the only one. The titanic Rockefeller Center used similar styling cues but applied them to what was basically an entire neighborhood. The style resulted in a catalogue of buildings, sculptures, frescos, and mosaics in which art and architecture joined hands to glorify the city's culture.

BOROUGHS AND NEIGHBORHOODS

Located at the mouth of the Hudson River, New York City spans out over several islands and part of the continent. Its most famous island is Manhattan, and the vastest is Long Island, whose western tip is part of the city, as it is home to Brooklyn and Queens. Staten Island is the most wild, and is located to the south, in the bay. Only the Bronx is not an island, but part of the continent. Up until 1898, there used to be five distinct cities. Manhattan, Brooklyn, Queens, the Bronx, and Staten Island. They then became boroughs, sort of official neighborhoods of one common city: New York.

Manhattan itself is generally divided into three major parts, from south to north: Downtown (up until 34th street), Midtown (from 34th to 59th street) and Uptown (from 59th to the Harlem River). In New York, the neighborhoods took on the names of their functions: the Financial District, or of their population: Chinatown or Little Italy, or of their geographic location: the Lower East Side and the Upper West Side. Others bear the names referring to their past, such as Greenwich Village, the East village, or Harlem. And some bear surprising names that New Yorkers created over time, such as Tribeca, an abbreviation of: The Triangle Below Canal Street; Soho for South of Houston; and Nolita for North of Little Italy. The same logic is applied to the other boroughs. Brooklyn has its Dumbo: Down Under the Manhattan Bridge Overpass, Queens has Little Egypt, and the Bronx has West Farms.

LOOKING AT DOWNTOWN SKYLINE FROM UNDER BROOKLYN BRIDGE, NEW YORK CITY

14808

THE STATUE OF LIBERTY
Liberty Island, Hudson River, Manhattan

In 1865, a French senator proposed the idea of a monument to celebrate the friendship between France and the United States. In honor of the Union's victory over the Confederacy in the Civil War, and the abolition of slavery that followed, the theme chosen for the monument was Liberty. Following a trip to New York, the sculptor in charge of the project, Frédéric Auguste Bartholdi, imagined an immense statue of a woman holding a torch: the future *Liberty Lighting the World*. The model was first cast in plaster, but the final structure was a metallic structure designed by Gustave Eiffel and built of copper panels. She was first built in Paris in 1884, before all 84 meters of her were dismantled for her shipment across the ocean. Due to a lack of financing, the pedestal, that the Americans were to build for her, was not yet ready. Lady Liberty had to wait in cargo containers before her arrival in the port of New York in June of 1885. She was finally inaugurated on October 28 1886. Draped in a toga like a Roman goddess, the monumental statue brandishes a torch and holds in her left hand the Declaration of Independence of July 4, 1776. Her bones weigh 125 tons and the copper skin another 100 tons. The inside is mostly hollow, and a spiral staircase of 354 steps takes you to the top of her crown. Today, she welcomes 4 million visitors per year.

102:—STATUE OF LIBERTY AT NIGHT. NEW YORK CITY.

1003

ELLIS ISLAND
Hudson River, Manhattan

By 1890, the constant influx of immigrants forced the federal government to build a temporary arrival station that would allow for the registration and documentation of the newly arrived immigrants. A stone's throw away from New Jersey, Ellis Island, located just north of Liberty Island, was chosen as the ideal location to welcome, hold, detain and possibly expel immigrants. The initial wooden building was quickly replaced by an elegant, French-renaissance styled building in brick and decorated with white stone. The architects' plan was such a success that it earned them a prize at the World Fair (*Exposition Universelle*) in Paris in 1900. The compound even included a hospital in order to isolate possible sick immigrants: 3,000 people died there during its operation. Upon their arrival, immigrants had to answer a questionnaire with twenty-nine questions, provide proof that they had sufficient funds to support themselves, and that they knew a trade or craft that would allow them to find work. They were also subjected to a thorough medical examination. Approximately 2% of applicants were rejected for criminal records, disease, mental illness, or a lack of qualifications, and summarily sent back to their homeland. At the peak of its activity, Ellis Island was processing and welcoming 5,000 people per day.

141.—ELLIS ISLAND, NEW YORK.

44521

NEW YORK HARBOUR
Hudson and East River

New York's location at the base of a protected bay and at the mouth of two rivers made it a natural port. It is in this haven that the sailor Giovanni da Verrazano threw his anchor when he discovered the region in 1524. One century later, the first dock was built on the East River, near the southern tip of the island of Manhattan. As the city grew, the port became increasingly important. Following the country's independence, it became the main port for trade between the United States and Europe. When the Erie Canal was dug, and the railroad system became more developed, it rose to the top of the list of ports in the New World. All along its banks, Manhattan became lined with numbered piers serving for trade shipment or passenger boats. Brooklyn also began to build shipyards, docks, and piers. Later, passenger ships docked nearly at the foot of skyscrapers. In the era between the two world wars, the French ship *The Normandie* and its rival ship *The Queen Mary* were regular star visitors. The former was requisitioned by the American army during World War II in 1941 and burned whiled docked in 1942. The latter, after serving to carry soldiers during the war, regained commercial service up until 1967. The legendary ship France arrived on its maiden voyage on February 8, 1962, at pier 88, where Normandie used to dock, along the Hudson. Today, cruise ships arrive at the same docks.

CASTLE CLINTON

Battery Park, Financial District, Manhattan

At the beginning of its colonization, the southern tip of Manhattan was a swamp-filled area. A short distance from the shore, Governor's Island was home to the Castle Williams fort, known as East Battery. On the western side, a rock formation was used to build the West Battery. These two artillery defense batteries were built between 1807 and 1811 in order to defend the city from any English attacks during the War of 1812. In 1817, the West Battery was renamed Castle Clinton in honor of the city's mayor. The patch of watery marsh that separated it from the island of Manhattan was progressively filled, creating a land bridge promenade called Battery Park. In 1823, the army transferred ownership of Castle Clinton to the city of New York. The fort was renovated and redesigned into a restaurant, called Castle Garden, hosting operas, theater, and even circus acts. But in 1855, the immigration boom pushed the city to place an arrival center for immigrants. It served as such up until 1890, when operations were transferred to Ellis Island. Eight million immigrants passed through it. In 1896, entertainment returned to the location, but in the form of the Aquarium of New York. Its star attraction, a Beluga whale, drew a crowd of over 30,000 people on opening day. The aquarium closed in 1941, and reopened at Coney Island in 1957. Since 1975, Castle Clinton is a national landmark.

Aquarium in Battery Park and New York Harbor.

STATEN ISLAND FERRY
Financial District, Manhattan

Everyday, eight boats carry approximately 100,000 people between Manhattan and State Island, the large, wild island located to the south of the Hudson's mouth, 8 kilometers from Manhattan. In the 18th century, it was reached via *periaugers*, flat-bottomed boats with two sails that served mostly for merchandise and cattle. The first steam boat entered into service in 1817, and was quickly bought by a certain Cornelius Vanderbilt, a native of the island who would go on to become one of the great magnates of New York. As of 1850, the ferry line became quite profitable, given the increasing and quick development of Staten Island. However, the boats were poorly maintained. On July 30, 1871, the steam engine of one such boat exploded while it was docked. Eighty-five people died and hundreds were injured. Jacob Vanderbilt, a descendant of Cornelius, was charged with murder. He escaped conviction, but ended up selling his boats to another company. In 1901, two boats collided and one sank to the harbor floor, taking with it five victims. The city had had enough. It seized the opportunity to take control of the ferry companies and turn them into a free public service. In 1909, the city inaugurated the massive Municipal Ferry Terminal, which remained in activity until damaged by fire in 1991.

DOWNTOWN SKYLINE FROM STATEN ISLAND FERRY, NEW YORK CITY

FRAUNCES TAVERN

Pearl Street, Financial District, Manhattan

In 1700, a French Huguenot named Étienne de Lancey (later Anglicized to Delancey) bought a lot at the corner of Pearl and Bond streets. In 1719, he had a brick building built and then rented it out. It hosted dance lessons and balls for the new bourgeoisie seeking a European form of glamour. It also was home to a company specializing in imports. Business was struggling, and so, in 1762, the building was sold to Samuel Fraunces, who turned it into a tavern. At the time, taverns served as a meeting place, for the exchange of ideas, and business negotiation, much like English clubs. The tavern also served traditional English fare. This didn't prevent the owner from also hosting the secret meetings of the Sons of Liberty, a group of rebels opposing British rule. Around the time of the Declaration of Independence, this group met regularly at the tavern, and Fraunces met George Washington. In 1783, when the British left New York, following their defeat, George Washington chose to celebrate his victory at Fraunces Tavern. The new administration even continued to meet there while awaiting completion of their new official buildings. In 1904, the Sons of the Revolution, a group of descendants of the original revolutionaries, bought the building and had it restore to its neo-colonial style that is still visible today.

Fraunces' Tavern. Broad & Pearl Sts., New York.

25865

ALEXANDER HAMILTON
US CUSTOM HOUSE
Bowling Green, Financial District, Manhattan

Among the first administrations created by the first Congress of the United States in 1789, none were as important for New York as the customs. It allowed for the collection of rights and taxes on all goods imported into the country, and also for the prosecution of contraband. In the century that followed independence, the US Customs service changed location a number of times. In 1892, the government decided to purchase a lot on the small park Bowling Green, halfway between the port and Wall Street. Cass Gilbert, who also built the Woolworth Building, was chosen as the architect for the project. He designed a building in the Beaux-Arts style, decorated with columns and allegory sculptures, the four main ones representing continents. The entrance is adorned with a great bald eagle, while the windows are decorated with heads representing the "eight races" of mankind. The interior contains several surprises as well, with a grand elliptical rotunda abundantly decorated with marble. In 1936, during the Great Depression, it received large murals painted by Reginald Marsh, an American painter born in Paris, known for depiction of port life in New York. The Customs service occupied the building from 1907 until 1971, when it moved to the World Trade Center. Since 1994, the building has been home to the National Museum of the American Indian.

3A-H1271

11

NEW YORK STOCK EXCHANGE
Broad Street, Financial District, Manhattan

The first stock market was located on Wall Street. It remained there until 1865, when it moved to Broad Street. Despite this change of address, the stock market continued to be referred to as Wall Street. In 1884, the stock exchange established a list of eleven important companies serving as a reference, known officially as the Dow Jones as of 1896. It was decided that to celebrate the success of the New York financial market, an appropriately grand building had to be built, taking the form of a Roman temple honoring capitalism: the New York Stock Exchange. The marble front was decorated with allegories representing Integrity protecting Commerce and Industry: values venerated by the American economy. The building was inaugurated in 1903. Today, its façade seems miniscule compared to the tall buildings that surround it. And yet, it is 17 stories tall! Every day, a bell announces the market opening. To ring it is considered an honor, granted since 1995 for such celebrities as Nelson Mandela and Kofi Annan, but also Snoop Dogg and fictional characters such as Mickey Mouse and Darth Vader.

NEW YORK STOCK EXCHANGE WALL STREET. NEW YORK CITY

WALL STREET
Financial District, Manhattan

The Dutch founded New Amsterdam in 1626. They protected their colony with a palisade that closed off the southern tip of Manhattan. When the English took over in 1664 and changed the name to New York, they replaced the wooden palisade with an actual wall. They quickly outgrew the small enclosure, and in 1699, they demolished the wall in order to facilitate traffic. The street that was built on the wall's trace took on its name: Wall Street. At the time, it crossed Manhattan from East to West: from the East River to the Hudson. It was a residential road, lined with beautiful houses and busy cafés. In 1711, a market for African and Indian slaves was opened. All sorts of transactions were carried out here. In the late 18th century, speculators and stockbrokers had taken the habit of meeting under a large button-wood tree for their financial transactions. In 1792, the most important among them signed the Buttonwood Agreement to regulate the city's stock market. At the same time, they started to meet at the Tontine Coffee House, one of the cafés on the street, launching the street's career as a business center. During the 19th century, the houses were replaced with skyscrapers. Only a few survived, like Federal Hall, where George Washington took his oath as first president of the United States, and Trinity Church.

WALL STREET
NEW YORK
CITY 1

PHOTO BY KEYSTONE

FEDERAL HALL
Wall Street, Financial District, Manhattan

During the American Revolution, New York was one of the last cities occupied by the British, despite the Declaration of Independence of 1776. The city would only be totally liberated in 1783. This did nothing to prevent it from imposing itself as capital of the new country. The brand new Federal Congress took up residence at City Hall built on Wall Street by the English. This is where the Constitution of the United States was drafted. The building was renamed Federal Hall, and it is where the constitution was ratified in 1788. The following year, on April 30, 1789, George Washington was sworn in on the balcony as first president of the United States of America. In 1790, however, other states of the Union were nervous about the cosmopolitan and business attitude of New Yorkers, and so preferred to transfer the federal capital to Philadelphia, a more populous city. Federal Hall was repurposed for municipal services, before being destroyed in 1812. The current building dates back to 1842. Built of light-colored marble like a Greek temple, and preceded by an imposing staircase, it first served as the Custom House. It then was home to the US Sub-Treasury, the predecessor to the Federal Reserve. The statue of George Washington in front of the colonnades was inaugurated in 1883, for the centennial celebration of the city's liberation. The building regained its former name of Federal Hall in 1939 when it was inscribed on the list of landmarks.

FINANCIAL CENTER, NEW YORK CITY

3A-H1274

TRINITY CHURCH
Broadway and Wall Street, Financial District,
Manhattan

Founded in 1697, Trinity Church was the first Anglican parish in New York. It swore allegiance to the King of England and paid him rent. Ravaged by fire and weather, two different sanctuaries took its place in the century that followed. In 1789, after national independence, the American branch of the Anglican Church became the Episcopal Church of the United States. Since 1976, it ordains women and even elected a lady bishop in 2006. When the current building was erected, between 1839 and 1846, it was the tallest building in the city, and its bell tower, at 87 meters high, was a landmark for sailors entering the port. In 1976, Queen Elizabeth II stopped by to receive 279 pepper grains (1 per year) as symbolic back pay for unpaid rent. The cemetery that surrounds the church holds tombs dating back to the 17th century. You would be mistaken to think that this is all that remains of the once vast properties given by the Crown to the parish. The modest garden is in fact the tip of a gigantic iceberg. Despite have sold several lots, Trinity Church remains one of the major real estate owners in Manhattan, with some 57,000 square meters of land, equaling 500,000 square meters of offices and businesses. The revenue generated by these properties makes it the richest parish in the world.

3A-H1299

TRINITY CHURCH AT BROADWAY AND WALL STREET, NEW YORK CITY

BROADWAY DOWNTOWN
Financial District and Civic Center, Manhattan

Broadway, the longest and most famous avenue of New York, crosses all of Manhattan's 21 kilometers, stretches 3 kilometers into Brooklyn, and even continues 29 kilometers north of New York, along the Hudson River, in the Westchester county. It's mostly known for its Midtown theaters, but it has very different faces depending on the neighborhood it crosses. Before the arrival of the colonial settlers, it was a path taken by Native Americans. The Dutch adopted it to connect their colony at the southern tip of Manhattan to the farms they had established at the northern part of the island. They nicknamed it Breede Weg (wide road), which the English adapted to Broad Way. In the 18th century, they called its southern portion Great George Street, in honor of their king. It was, at the time, the biggest avenue in the growing city. Over the years, the most prestigious buildings came to line its way, from Bowling Green park with the US Custom House in the south, to Trinity Church, St. Paul's Chapel, the Woolworth building and the new City Hall. Heading north, Broadway benefitted from urban expansion and was always an address for those wishing to impress. The first department stores opened shop along Broadway, before Fifth Avenue took the lion's share of that business.

AMERICAN TELEPHONE AND TELEGRAPH BUILDING
Broadway, Financial District, Manhattan

Also known by just its address, "195 Broadway", this 29-story building takes up an entire city block. Built in 1912 in a rigorous neo-classical style, it was planned as the headquarters of the American Telephone & Telegraph Company (known today as AT&T). Its architect, William Welles Bosworth, who had designed residences for Theodore Vail, the director of the company, and for John Rockefeller, was so proud of his building that he referred to it as his "temple on Broadway". He incorporated more marble in this building alone than any other building in New York. On the roof, he conceived handball and squash courts, surrounded by relaxation spaces with chaises longues. The small tower at one of the corners contained an immense bronze statue with gold leaf. It represented the Telegraph Genie, a winged boy carrying a cable and a lightning bolt, who was quickly nicknamed "Golden Boy". The AT&T building established the first transatlantic phone line, between New York and London, in 1927. The company left the building in 1984, but the statue stayed around until 1992, when the company moved once again, to New Jersey.

Telephone and Telegraph Building, New York City.

©W.J.ROEGE 23727

ST. PAUL'S CHAPEL
Broadway, Financial District, Manhattan

Along Broadway, the oldest church in Manhattan still active has survived all the catastrophes that devastated the city. It escaped all the fires, the worst of which, during the Revolutionary War, in 1776, destroyed Trinity Church, its mother church. During its construction in 1766, it was located in the midst of fields. The St. Martin-in-the-Fields Church in London inspired its sober neoclassical Georgian style. In the months that preceded the American Revolution, the Hearts of Oak militia, whose motto was "Liberty or Death" had the habit of meeting there, under the direction of Alexander Hamilton, one of the founding fathers of the United States. On the day of his inauguration as first president, George Washington came here to pray. It was also his church during the two years during which New York was the federal capital. In the days that followed the terrorist attacks of September 11, 2001, St. Paul's Chapel served as a refuge for the firemen and volunteer rescuers. Miraculously, the collapse of the two towers nearby caused no major damage to the chapel. Even the stained glass windows remained intact. However, the cloud of dust engulfed the cemetery, felled the trees, and entered the organ's pipes. In the days that followed, the fence around the church was covered in flowers and memorials to the victims of the attacks.

St. Paul Building & St. Paul Chapel, New York.

96-106

BARCLAY-VESEY BUILDING
Financial District, Manhattan

Erected between 1922 and 1927 under the direction of the architect Ralph Walker, this building is considered to be the first Art Deco skyscraper in New York. Reaching 32 floors, it was designed to host the offices of five thousand employees. As it reaches higher and higher, the building gets thinner and thinner, with its staggered architecture that allows it to avoid the "canyon effect" that its neighboring monoliths imposed on the streets below. Walker also used styling cues that were typically Art Deco, for example by incorporating natural elements such as leaves, animals, and babies around a bell in reference to the phone company that commissioned the building. His design, which he claimed was inspired by Mayan architecture, was considered to be a great innovation. As a result, he received the gold medal from the Architectural League of New York in 1927. At the time, the Barclay-Vesey building looked out directly on the Hudson River and its docks. Since then, that area has become densely urbanized. The building drew its nickname from the two streets that frame it to the north and south: Barclay and Vesey Streets. The hall that crosses the entire building is lined with bronze plaques that retrace the history of the New York telephone network, and the ceiling is painted with murals depicting the history of communication. Since 2009, the Barclay-Vesey building is a landmark.

WOOLWORTH BUILDING
Broadway, Civic Center, Manhattan

Who could have imagined that the owner of a chain of discount-price stores would one day have the means to build the tallest skyscraper in New York? It is a testament to the ambition of Frank Woolworth, who opened his first shop in 1878, and who by 1911 owned 586 stores. He wished to house his company headquarters in a building that represented his new fortune, and so purchased a lot of land almost across the street from City Hall. The project was entrusted to Cass Gilbert, who was already famous for having designed the US Custom House. To build what he conceived as a "cathedral of commerce", Woolworth wanted a neo-gothic style rich in detailed stonework, gargoyles, and pinnacles. The first stone was laid in August of 1911, and the inauguration took place in April 1913, after less than years at a rate of one and a half stories per week. To celebrate the event, the President of the United States himself lit the building's 80,000 light bulbs at once, from the White House! The hall, in the form of a Latin cross three stories high, vaulted and covered in mosaics and murals perfectly evokes the cathedral that its owner had hoped for. Topping out at 241 meters, the Woolworth Building was the highest skyscraper in the city and the world, and remained so until 1930. Always a showoff, the owner paid in one go and in cash the approximately 15.5 million dollars that the building cost him.

Woolworth Building and Broadway Looking North,

New York City.

PARK ROW BUILDING
Park Row, Civic Center, Manhattan

In the 19th century, Park Row, the street that ran along City Hall, was always very busy. It bordered the business center and led to the Brooklyn Bridge. It's where press companies progressively began to set up shop (*New York World*, *New York Sun*, *New York Tribune*, *New York Times, etc.*), which lent the street the nickname Paper Row. The most imposing building of the street, the Park Row Building, erected in 1899, was home to the offices of the Associated Press, a newspaper coop founded established in 1846.It was one of the first skyscrapers with a metal structure, allowing it to be fifteen or even twenty stories taller than all the neighboring buildings. Its massive façade and two towers crowned with domes were unmatched in New York. At 119 meters, it was the tallest building in the world and kept this record until 1908. Eight thousand tons of steel were used in its structure. The result, with its heavy appearance, did not win over the public opinion. The press was not convinced, and called it "a monster". On the side facing City Hall, four statues decorate the fifth floor. Inside, ten elevators, arranged in an arc, service the 29 floors divided into 950 offices each planned for four employees. Today, the Park Row Building, which has barely changed, maintains its initial purpose.

CITY HALL
Civic Center, Manhattan

After the Declaration of Independence in 1776, the city began to erect public buildings. The former City Hall on Wall Street had become Federal Hall, and so there was need for a new one. Along Broadway, a lot that had formerly been a prison and gallows during the Revolutionary War was selected. The project began in 1800, and two years later, an architectural contest was held. Two winners were selected: the Frenchman Joseph-François Mangin, as the main architect and the Scotsman John McComb, as deputy and supervisor. The collaboration between these two architects resulted in a mix of French neo-renaissance and American federal style. At the time, the building was located at the northern part of the city. It was decided that the façade should look towards the city, and nobody imagined that the city might continue to extend greatly towards the north. The part facing the city was built using white marble from Massachusetts, but due to limited funds, the back, facing what was back then countryside, was build using much less expensive sandstone. The construction lasted ten years, due to project finance problems and even a yellow fever epidemic.

City Hall was finally opened to the public in 1812. Today, its park is a favorite lunch spot of employees from the neighboring business area.

Greater New York Souvenir

CITY HALL

N.Y. WORLD

MUNICIPAL BUILDING
Center Street, Civic Center, Manhattan

The construction of this building coincided with the unification of the five boroughs into one city in 1898. It last from 1907 to 1915. The sheer size of the building required complex planning, especially since for the first time, a building was to incorporate a subway station. The architects imagined a building in a Beaux-Arts style, but its gigantic proportions can make one forget the delicate touch of neoclassicism. It is one of the largest administrative buildings in the world. The lower part of the building is lined with tall columns that frame an arch of triumph inspired by Constantine's in Rome, that leads to a central square. In this skyscraper, everything is superlative, right up to the tower that decorates its center: it looks miniscule but is actually fifteen-stories high! At the top, a golden statue guards a bell eight meters tall, called Civic Fame, who holds a crown with five points, one for each borough of the city. WNYC public radio, one of the oldest in the country, starting broadcasting from the roof of the building in 1937. It was the first to announce the Japanese attack of Pearl Harbor in 1941. Today, the Municipal Building hosts more than three thousand public workers and an average of eighty weddings are held there every day.

BROOKLYN BRIDGE
Civic Center, Manhattan and Dumbo, Brooklyn

Before 1850, crossing the East River required a ferry. In 1857, the construction of a bridge was evoked, but was only launched in 1869. John Roebling, the engineer who had created the bridge at Niagara Falls was put in charge, but died in an accident at the site shortly after construction began. His son replaced him, but the delays multiplied: the too-hard bedrock of the river, the requirement to work underwater in poorly adapted pressurized caissons, the complex suspension system all set back the completion. The bridge took thirteen years to be built and was inaugurated in 1883. Twenty-seven workers lost their life to the project and many others suffered from burst eardrums due to the underwater work.

1825 meters long, the structure is balanced on two neogothic granite arches that reach 48 meters above the road. The central portion of the bridge, 486 meters long, is held up by enormous cables, the widest of which is 40 centimeters in diameter. The bridge is 41 meters above the waters of the East River. On the day of the inauguration, over 150,000 pedestrians and 8,000 vehicles rushed to cross it. The first to cross it, however, was Emily Roebling, the widow of the bridge's designer.

35 — BROOKLYN BRIDGE AT NIGHT, NEW YORK CITY

PELL STREET
Chinatown, Manhattan

Chinese immigration began in 1858 with the arrival of a Cantonese man who began to sell cigars near City Hall. Living near Chatham Square, this salesman then proceeded to rent out beds to his newly arrived fellow compatriots, beginning what would become Chinatown. He encourage them to also get into the cigar-selling business, which quickly became the specialty of the Chinese neighborhood, between Mott Street, Pell Street, and Doyers Street. In 1870 there were still only about 200 Chinese immigrants in the city. The numbers greatly increased ten years later, when many arrived from the Western part of the United States, where the emptied out gold mines had left them unemployed. At the end of the 1880's, they were close to 10,000 in Manhattan- mostly single men. They were piled into sordid rooms rented for low prices. Gambling, opium dens, and brothels made up the majority of the tiny neighborhood. On Pell Street, the Chinese opened or took over restaurants, one of which, the famous and chic Chinese Delmonico, was the meeting spot for secret clubs and gangs. Today, Chinatown is still mostly populated by the Cantonese, while the newer arrivals from the province of Fujian have stretched the neighborhood to the east, encroaching on traditionally Jewish and Hispanic areas.

549:—PELL STREET (CHINATOWN), NEW YORK CITY.

MOTT STREET
Chinatown, Manhattan

———

Mott Street is the commercial throughway of Chinatown. Along with the metal fire-escape staircases, the brick building façades are covered in signs in Chinese characters. The street was first built in the 18th century, lining a freshwater reservoir that used to supply the city. As New York grew, several industries appeared in the area, including tanneries, breweries, and slaughterhouses. But the pollution they caused led the reservoir to be closed and filled up in the early 19th century. In 1893, On Leong Tong took over the street. This secret Chinese society of Chinese businessmen controlled gambling and racketed the neighborhood businesses. It also actively and violently participated in the New York gang wars. In the early 20th century, Hip Sing Tong, specialized in the drug trafficking, began to compete. This mafia brotherhood was joined by an offshoot of Lung Kong Tin Yee from San Francisco and known as the Four Brothers Gang. The gang wars affected the neighborhood for many years; they culminated in the 1970's, when a new group from Hong Kong and Taiwan, the Ghost Shadows, took control of Mott Street and focused on illegal betting, drugs, and racketeering.

———

MOTT STREET, CHINATOWN, NEW YORK CITY.

26060

CHATHAM SQUARE
Chinatown, Manhattan

As one of the entrances to Chinatown, this square is invaded today by streams of cars, and yet once had a turbulent history. Located northeast of the City Hall, it was originally considered a peaceful place. New Yorkers came here for the large market with many fruits and vegetables as well as horses or cattle. This tranquility did not continue after the urban explosion and the influx of new immigrants who crowded into this part of Manhattan close to the port and shipyards. Italians and Irish fought over every inch. A sprawling slum had developed around Chatham Square, the famous area of Five Points, represented in the film by Martin Scorsese, *Gangs of New York*. Epidemics, interracial fights, heinous crimes, clashes between rival gangs afflicted the neighborhood. Chatham Square was full of only dubious bars and tattoo salons. The arrival of the Chinese and the violence of the new gangs worsened the situation. The slum was gradually dismantled during the second half of the nineteenth century, but the area did not improve. Chatham Square, where eight different streets meet, became a railway junction where two overhead railway lines crossed. After closing these lines in 1942 and 1955, the square was completely redesigned. An arch was erected there in memory of the Chinese soldiers who died for the United States.

Chatham Square and Bowery, New York City.

MANHATTAN BRIDGE
Chinatown, Manhattan and Dumbo, Brooklyn

The Manhattan Bridge was the last of three bridges built above the East River between Manhattan and Brooklyn. Its construction was decided in 1901. In 1909 it was already partially open to the public, with wooden boards placed astride the steel beams. Work was not fully completed until three years later when the trains were able to cross it. It now had eight railway tracks and lanes for cars and others for pedestrians. Its painted blue steel towers rise up to 102 meters and the total length of the bridge is 2090 meters. At 448 meters in length, the central portion is shorter than the Brooklyn Bridge by 38 meters. Its main cables are about 54 centimeters in diameter and are made of 9472 wires each. The Manhattan-side access makes it a unique bridge. Designed by Carrère and Hastings, the architects of the New York Public Library, it consists of a triumphal arch 22 meters high, inspired by the Porte Saint-Denis in Paris and framed on either side by a double ellipse colonnade forming an elegant square. Manhattan Bridge connects Chinatown on the Manhattan side and Dumbo, on the Brooklyn side. Today, 450,000 people pass through it on a daily basis, of which 4,000 cyclists, more than 85,000 vehicles and 950 subways or commuter trains.

66:—Manhattan Bridge Approach, New York.

WILLIAMSBURGH BRIDGE

Lower East Side, Manhattan
and Williamsburg, Brooklyn

The Williamsburg Bridge was the second bridge built over the East River, between Manhattan and Brooklyn. At the time of its inauguration in 1903, it was the longest suspension bridge in the world, thanks to its central portion measuring 490 meters. It was also the most original in the city, thanks to its lattice design, a technique that appeared in the US in the mid-nineteenth century: metal girders, vertical and diagonal, intersect to form the superstructure and maintain the deck without support cables. Although built twenty years afterwards, the Williamsburg Bridge cost $1 million less than the Brooklyn Bridge, and its construction took six years less. One of its features is that it connects two traditionally Jewish neighborhoods, the Lower East Side on the Manhattan side, and Hassidic neighborhood of Broadway on the Brooklyn side. Every day, some of the inhabitants of Brooklyn, wearing their large black hats, cross to go to work in Manhattan. It is now one of the most beautiful crossings of the East River, particularly popular with cyclists and roller-bladers who enjoy the calm. Jazz great Sonny Rollins succumbed to its charm: in the late 1950s, when he went through a serious personal crisis, he disappeared from the public scene and spent two years playing the saxophone for hours, alone under beams of the Williamsburg Bridge.

NEW YORK. The Williamsburgh Bridge.

WASHINGTON SQUARE
West Village, Manhattan

In 1827, a green space was designed in the neighborhood of the new wealthy homes beginning to appear in the area. The lot had previously served as a pillory. Four years later, the prestigious New York University, NYU, which prides itself for many Nobel and Pulitzer prizes, was founded next to this park. It attracted the elite of the city becoming one of the epicenters of New York intellectual life. This elegant park today serves as a hinge between the bohemian artist in Greenwich Village and the bourgeoisie of chic 5th Avenue. Washington Arch, a triumphal arch erected to celebrate the centenary of George Washington's inauguration as the first president of the United States, borders its north side, facing 5th Avenue. On the south side, the park opens on Thompson and Sullivan Streets, full of jazz bars and cafes. Writers Henry James and Edith Wharton both resided nearby. The neighborhood also counted the painter Edward Hopper and a whole avant-garde community: from Dylan Thomas to Ernest Hemingway and John Dos Passos, from Marcel Duchamp to Jackson Pollock and Mark Rothko. It is also a den of chess players: for decades, they meet under the trees at the southwest corner of the park in two nearby streets, lending this micro-district the nickname Chess Distric.

COOPER SQUARE
East Village, Manhattan

This East Village square is located north of the Bowery, the large avenue of lower Manhattan. In 1850, the neighborhood was rather bourgeois, thanks to the investments of wealthy New York families like the Astors. The neighborhood included Astor Opera House and the Astor Library. This great crossroads owes its identity though to a certain Peter Cooper. This industrialist and philanthropist decided in 1859 to found an institution of higher education, whose brick building still dominates the area. The son of a worker, a self-taught genius, Cooper made his fortune through his many inventions, from a machine to cut fabric to the first steam locomotive and gelatin. Its aim was to provide free classes for adults evening, regardless of race, religion or sex, to offer each determined individual the possibility of getting an education. The property, The Cooper Union, later gave birth to several specialized schools, including architecture, technical studies, and the arts. Thomas Edison was one of the most famous students. In 1878, Cooper Square was disfigured by the construction of the aboveground subway tracks on 3rd Avenue. In 1955, a new resident settled in: the weekly The Village Voice, launched to offer a cultural alternative to traditional large newspapers. Sassy and controversial, the paper opened its pages to writers like Henry Miller and Allen Ginsberg.

COOPER SQUARE BY NIGHT, NEW YORK

1993

GENERAL POST OFFICE
8th Avenue and 31st Street, Chelsea, Manhattan

Among the most pompous public buildings, the General Post Office holds a prominent position: it occupies 32,000 square meters! Its massive Beaux-Arts style is adorned with Corinthian columns, imposing flights of stairs and coffered ceilings. Built between 1912 and 1914, it was assorted with the front of Pennsylvania Station, the train station across the street. The architect firm chosen for these two buildings, McKim, Mead & White, was one of the most reputable US firms, which gave us the campus of Columbia University and the Brooklyn Museum. The proximity of the station allowed the mail to arrive quickly and was easier to transport. The façade of the post office clearly shows its mission in a motto carved in stone: «Neither snow nor rain nor heat nor gloom of night stays these couriers from the swift completion of their appointed rounds.» This phrase was inspired by the description given by Herodotus of the horseback messenger service of Xerxes, king of Persia in ancient times. It was engraved by Ira Schnapp, a young man of nineteen who drew and engraved stamps. Subsequently, he became the designer of Action Comics, the periodical comic book that launched Superman. In 1963, the Pennsylvania Station building was demolished, and the station transferred underground.

GENERAL POST OFFICE BUILDING, 8TH AVENUE & 31ST STREET, NEW YORK CITY

14806

HOTEL PENNSYLVANIA
7th Avenue, Chelsea, Manhattan

In 1919, the Pennsylvania Railroad Company decided to open a gigantic hotel to accommodate streams of travelers that its trains were spilling onto New York. To design the building, which would stand opposite the entrance from Pennsylvania Station, the architect firm McKim, Mead & White was called upon, as they were the architects of the General Post Office. An advert, published in 1919, praised the opening of the largest hotel in the world: two thousand two hundred room on twenty-seven floors, and the height of modernity, just as many bathrooms! It surpassed its rival, the Commodore Hotel, which itself had only... two thousand rooms. For light to enter a larger number of rooms, the building was divided into four identical towers above the base formed by the first floors. For the comfort of guests, each room came with a «servidor», a closet with a double opening on the bedroom and hallway. It was possible to deposit shoes or clothes at night and activate an electric signal for an employee to pick up the items and return them cleaned the next morning. Any room service order could be delivered in the same manner discreetly. As for the main café in the establishment, it offered a gothic décor with vaulted ceilings and stained glass windows worthy of a chapel. Since 1997, the Pennsylvania narrowly escaped demolition several times, and its future remains uncertain.

FLATIRON BUILDING

Broadway and 5th Avenue, Flatiron District, Manhattan

The sharp triangle profile of this building earned it the nickname "Flatiron". It owes its peculiarity to the triangular shape of the land on which it is built at the intersection of 5th Avenue and Broadway. The plans were entrusted to Daniel Burnham, an architect from Chicago, where at the time an innovative architectural style based on steel structures was being developed. For the Flatiron, he imagined a very ornate Italian Renaissance style, with innumerable windows and a multitude of ledges. The metal frame was prefabricated, allowing mounting the floors quickly. The construction took only a year, and the building of twenty-one stories was inaugurated in June of 1902. The result was of a rare elegance and offered a staggering perspective. Despite its height of 87 meters, the thin bow of the building measures just 6 feet! At the time of its construction, the public was quickly seduced by what was to become one of the icons of the city. The critique, including architects, however, was very doubtful. The New York Tribune spoke of a «meager slice of cake,» while the New York Times spoke of it as a «monstrosity.» It was only when artists and intellectuals, such as photographers Edward Steichen and Alfred Stiglitz or the writer HG Wells, used its curious profile that it became recognized as a genuine work of art.

METROPOLITAN LIFE
INSURANCE TOWER
Flatiron District, Manhattan

On the corner of Madison Square, this high tower is a later addition to a building built in 1893 for an insurance company. The architect of the building was Napoleon Le Brun. In 1905, when the company decided to expand its headquarters, it once again called on him. Rather than adding a few floors, the architect opted for a corner tower, in the manner of an Italian Renaissance-style belfry. The campanile of St Mark's Basilica in Venice inspired it. He reproduced it through significant inflation in size: it measures 213 meters and has fifty floors. For good measure, he also copied Big Ben by adding a clock on each side. Each dial is 8 meters in diameter, with figures of 1.20 meters high and needles weighing between 350 and 500 kilos! The tower remained the highest in the world until the construction of the Woolworth Building. Meanwhile, on the inside, Newell Wyeth was entrusted with making fourteen large murals for which he was paid $ 50 per square meter. His employers had no idea he would become one of the most popular illustrators of his time working for Coca-Cola, Lucky Strike and many publishers. In 1964 the tower was brutally renovated with the suppression of original ornaments and the marble was replaced with a veneer of gray stone. In 2015, it was converted into a hotel.

The Metropolitan Life Insurance Building, New York

MADISON SQUARE
NoMad, Manhattan

Before the extension of New York, this part of Manhattan was occupied by wetlands. At the beginning of the eighteenth century, this is where the poor were buried. In the decades that followed, the area served as a military training ground. It included an arsenal and a reformatory for delinquent children. At the corner of the future 5th Avenue and 23rd Street, an inn served as a stopover for travelers heading north. It was demolished in 1853 to make way for a racetrack. The park itself was created in 1847. The Fifth Avenue Hotel, the first hotel with lifts, opened its doors on the west side in 1859. Theaters and private clubs appeared in the area. But all this excitement drove away the bourgeois residents, who sought quiet and the neighborhood changed dramatically. The sandstone houses gave way to department stores. There were so many that the stretch of 5th Avenue south to Madison Square was nicknamed the Ladies Mile. The park was renovated and refurbished in 1870. In the east, Madison Square Garden was opened in 1879 to host the Westminster Kennel Club Dog Show, a famous canine contest, boxing matches and sporting events. An eponymous covered arena room replaced it in 1890, but was demolished in 1926 to move further north, where it still exists.

MADISON SQUARE, METROPOLITAN LIFE AND FLAT IRON BUILDINGS, NEW YORK CITY.

HERALD SQUARE
Garment District, Manhattan

This lively intersection is at the crossroads of Broadway and 6th Avenue with 34th Street. It is named after the New York Herald newspaper, which had opened here in the late nineteenth century. In 1921 the building was demolished. The two bronze owls that decorated the building were preserved and today are used to decorate the square. Besides its high concentration of press offices, Herald Square was also the gateway to the Garment District. The apparel industry is linked to the history of New York. With the arrival of mechanization, it left the small family workshops of the Jewish Lower East Side, where it had started at the beginning of the nineteenth century. It settled in Midtown, close to shops that were growing in number. The large Jewish immigration from Central and Eastern Europe fueled cheap labor to this industry, which became the city's main business at the turn of the twentieth century. Among the main contractors were the great historic New York stores such as Lord & Taylor and Brooks Brothers, suppliers of uniforms of all kinds that were not far, on 5th and Madison Avenues. As for the famous Macy's, another important partner, it is still on Herald Square. Since the 1960's, a portion of 32nd Street, east of Herald Square, is home to a Korean community, and is now nicknamed Koreatown.

Herald Square, Where Broadway Meets Sixth Avenue

MACY'S
Herald Square, Garment District, Manhattan

"The biggest store in the world" is proudly written on Macy's façade looking out on the Herald Square. Long before reaching that point, the company began as a simple general store, hardware store, which was opened in 1843 in Massachusetts by Rowland Macy, a former whaling captain. His first New York store, created in 1858, was in the southern part of Manhattan. The business prospered, and became a real department store. In 1902, feeling that Midtown would become a more favorable area, the Macy's firm decided to move its address to Herald Square. But it was a bet on the future. The shop used a steam-powered wagon to pick up customers at the old location. Fuller Company, a Chicago construction company that was invested at the time in the building of Flatiron Madison Square, supervised construction of the new building. The Palladian style of the ten-story building remained sober, but was enlivened with successive extensions incorporating Art Deco details. Macy's distinguished itself by its aggressive advertising, such as the tradition of placing huge posters on the building dating back to 1945. Today, the store is especially popular in New York for the Thanksgiving Day Parade, a spectacular parade of floats, and for its fireworks show on July 4th of every year.

HERALD SQUARE

NEW YORK

209

LINCOLN TUNNEL
Garment District, Manhattan, and Weehawken, New Jersey

Crossing the Hudson, to the west of Manhattan, presented several difficulties, as the river is very wide. Railway tunnels existed since the early twentieth century to connect Manhattan to New Jersey by train, but cars had to take the ferry. A first road tunnel, the Holland Tunnel, opened in 1927, from Lower Manhattan. The second, the Lincoln Tunnel, was to connect Midtown with Weehawken, New Jersey. The initial project involved two separate tunnels, each with two lanes. Begun in 1934, the first was completed in just over three years and inaugurated in December 1937. Construction of the second was interrupted by the arrival of the war and the shortage of metal. It opened in 1945. The increase in car traffic quickly saturated the four lanes, which raised the project of a third tunnel, which went into service in 1957. The success of the Lincoln Tunnel never wavered: one hundred and twenty thousand vehicles use it per day, making it one of the busiest in the world. A special feature: only the crossing into Manhattan is subject to a toll. The Lincoln Tunnel, like its neighbor the Holland Tunnel, is considered sensitive targets for terrorism and as such is subject to special surveillance.

Entrance to Lincoln Tunnel, New York City

14

PHOTO BY KEYSTONE

SLOW

EMPIRE STATE BUILDING
5th Avenue, Garment District, Manhattan

Designed before the stock market crash of 1929, this skyscraper entered the fierce competition for the highest building in the city. The car manufacturer Chrysler was then about to smash the record. Never mind, the boss of General Motors would win the challenge! At 381 meters high, the Empire State Building would surpass its rival by over 120 meters and remain unrivaled until the construction of the World Trade Center in 1970. On the architectural front, they opted for an austere Art Deco style, far different from the exuberant gleaming Chrysler Building. Only the hall, three floors high and with polychrome marble, yielded to opulence. The crisis of 1929, which broke out as construction began, discouraged no one. On the contrary, construction broke all speed records: the building was completed in one year and forty-five days, at the rate of four floors per week. Of the three thousand builders working in perilous conditions, five lost their life. The Empire State Building opened in 1931. Two years later, the movie King Kong featured a giant gorilla climbing to the top of the skyscraper, which raised the building to the status of mythical symbol of the city. Sixty-seven elevators service the building but the ultimate is to try the annual «run-up»: 1,576 steps that the best climb in less than ten minutes!

HOTEL VANDERBILT

Park Avenue and 34th Street, Murray Hill, Manhattan

In the early twentieth century, wealthy New York families who did not know how to spend their money often threw it into the construction of hotels. The Astors were among the richest, but the Vanderbilt family, who made its fortune in railroads, was not far behind. After having built Grand Central Station in 1911, Alfred Vanderbilt thought to use the services of the same architects Warren & Wetmore, to build a hotel that would rival the Waldorf Astoria or the St. Regis. Their choice was a replica, more massive, in the neoclassical Adam style popular in England in the eighteenth century. The twenty-two floors and three towering wings of the building mesmerized passersby. The terracotta decoration was discreet decor, and the interior was equipped with the best modern comforts such as pneumatic tubes that allowed delivery of messages to the top floor in seven seconds! Rather than just the tourist clientele, Vanderbilt was targeting long-term guests, to whom he offered an understated elegance. Besides, he had himself moved into the top two floors of the hotel. Among the famous guests, the hotel counted the tenor Enrico Caruso and Howard Hughes Jr., a terribly wayward billionaire. Alfred Vanderbilt did not get to enjoy his beautiful apartment for very long. He died during the sinking of the Lusitania, torpedoed by the Germans in 1915.

HOTEL VANDERBILT, 34TH ST. & PARK AVE., NEW YORK

TIMES SQUARE
Theater District, Manhattan

In the early nineteenth century when the area still smelled like the countryside, the wealthy John Astor began buying land in this area called Long Acre. The main activity was stagecoach and carriages industry along Broadway. William Vanderbilt, another millionaire, also managed the horse market there. At the turn of the twentieth century, the place was rowdy because the popular theaters and brothels that multiplied to the north of Madison Square brought their share of shady characters. Then in 1904, the New York Times came and settled here. Long Acre was soon renamed Times Square in its honor. Visionary, the newspaper's owner managed to persuade the mayor to build a metro station, which soon became the main public transport mode of New York. Gradually, the prospering theaters made Times Square a huge garish forum. With the Great Depression, the area gradually acquired a terrible reputation for violence and corruption. Sex shops and hostess bars swarmed, leading the area into a slow decline. It was not until the 1980s that it became the symbol of the hectic New York success, a kaleidoscope of glittering neon lights, with the most symbolic: the giant Nasdaq screen that displays real-time stock prices on the market.

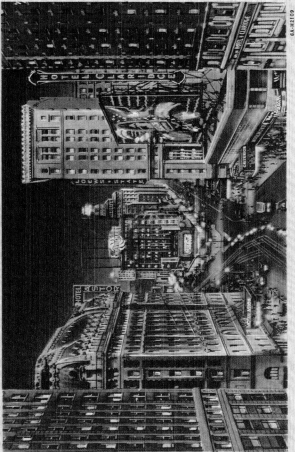

6A-H2109

ONE TIMES SQUARE
Times Square, Theater District, Manhattan

Built in 1904 to house the New York Times, the Times Building sits at number 1 on the street, which earned it the nickname "One Times Square." At 120 meters high, this narrow building that hugs the diagonal crossing of Broadway and 7th Avenue dominated the neighborhood at the time of its construction. Adolph Ochs, the charismatic director of the Times, succeeded in getting the district to be named after his newspaper. To win public support, he launched, at the 1904 New Year's Eve, the tradition of celebrating the stroke of midnight with fireworks. To ring in 1908, he had another idea: that of a big ball lit by a hundred bulbs that slowly descended during a count of sixty seconds leading up to midnight. The tradition of coming to see it each December 31 continues today. In 1913, the newspaper moved nearby, but kept the building for its advertising and communication services. The use of electricity to communicate is a constant in the history of the Times Building. In 1928, to share the results of the presidential election, a news ticker was installed above the ground floor, a luminous panel that paraded the information almost in real time. Giant electrical advertisements eventually completely covered the front of One Times Square, which brings in nearly $ 25 million in annual revenue.

Times Building, New York City.

BROADWAY MIDTOWN
Theater District, Manhattan

Broadway's endless journey through Manhattan lends this mythical avenue many different profiles depending on the neighborhood, from the Downtown office buildings to the shops and homes of the Upper West Side. In the popular imagination, it is synonymous with Broadway theater, festivals and musicals. And yet the reality behind this reputation only takes up a small portion of the avenue, around Times Square. This is where we find the bright posters of shows that are sometimes played for decades. The arrival of theaters and concert halls in the neighborhood began in the early twentieth century and boomed in the 1920's, though they were not limited to Broadway, but over eighty establishments spread out on perpendicular streets, between 6th and 8th Avenues. Many restaurants, hotels and cafes came to complete the festive offer. The majority of the shows produced by the forty professional theaters still in operation now focuses on musicals that made Broadway famous. Disney realized this, and became one of the most important investors, with hits that are exported worldwide. Other shows are also part of the cultural history of the country, as was the case of *West Side Story* or the very commercial *Phantom of the Opera*, performed since January 1988.

NEW YORK

PARAMOUNT BUILDING

Broadway and 44th Street, Theater District, Manhattan

In the 1920s, the boom of cinema led to the opening of many film theaters in the Times Square area. In 1926, Paramount Pictures began to build its headquarters on Broadway, between 43rd and 44th Streets. Its boss, Adolph Zukor, wanted to showcase his business. Apart from offices, the building was to have a theater. The project was entrusted to an architectural firm in Chicago that opted for an Art Deco style. The building was topped with a pyramid with steps to evoke the idea of a mountain, the symbol of Paramount. The facade was decorated with a huge clock whose numbers are five-pointed stars, recalling the famous starry circle logo of the company. At the top, a glass globe lit up the night. The interior decoration was just as grand: a profusion of gilding and statues, frescoed ceilings...the neo-Renaissance facade of the theater, in the back, hiding a hall copied on that of the Garnier Opera House in Paris. The room housed 3664 seats and presented concerts, live shows and movies. Over the years, many celebrities performed at the Paramount Theater: from Benny Goodman to the Andrews Sisters, from Frank Sinatra to Jerry Lewis. It closed in 1966. The main building, on Broadway, still exists. It is listed as a landmark since 1988 and houses offices, as well as the Hard Rock Cafe.

608:—THE PARAMOUNT BROADWAY BUILDING,

© BROWN BROS.

NEW YORK CITY

FIFTH AVENUE
Midtown, Manhattan

The route of the 5th Avenue appeared on city maps in 1911. At that time, the avenue was still a single dirt road lined with farms and country houses, which connected what became Washington Square in the south to the Harlem River in the north. The Brevoorts, descendants of Dutch farmers, owned extensive grounds along it. In 1934, Henry Brevoort built himself a mansion in the southern part of the 5th Avenue, kicking off its urbanization. Other wealthy families gradually followed suit such as the Renwicks, the Astors, the Vanderbilts... The chic fate of the avenue seemed sealed. The construction of the first Waldorf Astoria hotel in 1893, next to the residence of Caroline Astor, on a site now occupied by the Empire State Building, marked a major turning point. As the avenue grew northward, discrete brownstone mansions mingled with grandiose châteaux and increasingly conspicuous hotels. The presence of high society in the neighborhood encouraged the opening of luxury stores such as Lord & Taylor, which still exists. Today it is still the part of the 5th Avenue that extends from 34th to 60th Street, which has the highest concentration of luxury brands, like Tiffany & Co.

3A-H1289

NEW YORK PUBLIC LIBRARY

5th Avenue and 42nd Street, Midtown West, Manhattan

This large public library, with over twenty million books, is probably the most prestigious example of Beaux-Arts in New York. It was at the Beaux-Arts School in Paris that most American architects studied, from the Independence to the Great Depression. They brought forth eclecticism with a taste for mixtures of European styles from neoclassical to neo-Gothic. The New York Public Library, designed in 1902 by the firm Carrère & Hastings, mingled French architectural styles. As is often the case for American cultural institutions, it came to fruition thanks to generous patrons of the city. During the second half of the nineteenth century, two billionaires, John Jacob Astor and James Lenox, each had left their collections of books to create libraries, but these faced financial difficulties. In 1886, Samuel Tilden, a philanthropic politician bequeathed the bulk of his fortune for building a free public library. His executor had the good idea of bringing together the Astor and Lenox libraries to offer a unique catalog. Tilden's money financed the construction of building on 5th Avenue, completed in 1910. It took a year to move and install all the books on the approximately 121 km of shelves. The President of the United States inaugurated the library in 1911.

3A-H1289

ROCKEFELLER CENTER
Midtown West, Manhattan

Among the great philanthropists who made New York, John D. Rockefeller Junior was the most prominent; an oil tycoon and the richest man in the world. In 1910, he left the family business to devote himself to the management of its assets and patronage. He was excellent in business matters, and he also spent a great deal of his money on social and cultural causes. For example, he offered the land to build the UN headquarters. He also built the MoMA. Despite a long list of prestigious projects, the symbol of his commitment remains Rockefeller Center. Other businessmen had built skyscrapers, but none had imagined an urban complex of this magnitude, both by size and by its avant-garde style. From the initial draft of a space for the Metropolitan Opera, it is a city within a city that was finally born. A set of thirteen buildings, connected by an underground mall, surrounding a central square crowned with the iconic skyscraper that would dominate Manhattan. Above all, the concept rested in the consistency of the proposed style, the ultimate of Art Deco, with each perspective, each element of decor, devised to integrate into a global picture. Construction began in 1931, at the height of the depression, and Rockefeller Center was not fully completed until the 1970s.

NEW YORK CITY

14853

RCA BUILDING
6th Avenue, Midtown West, Manhattan

Known as the General Electric Building, but nicknamed «The Rock», this skyscraper built for the RCA (Radio Corporation of America) is the flagship of Rockefeller Center. 260 meters high, it has seventy floors. Completed in 1933, after less than sixteen months of work, this Art Deco gem was designed by the architect Raymond Hood, one of the stars of this style in the US. Seen from the ground, this assembly of parallel vertical lines accentuates the impression of height and finesse. The terrace, called «Top of the Rock» offers a breathtaking view of all Manhattan. The Rock is also distinguished by its decor, which boasts the knowledge of a secular religion. The exterior is decorated with reliefs evoking wisdom through a Bible verse. On the 6th Avenue side, a huge mosaic, entitled *Intelligence Awakening Mankind* shows the victory of knowledge over poverty and fear. The huge hall is adorned with monumental frescoes, *American Progress*, which revisits the mythology and portrays the birth of the United States. Originally, the work was entrusted to the Mexican muralist Diego Rivera. But the painter, a fervent communist, had a vision of progress too Marxist for his sponsors: he had worked into his fresco scenes from May 1 of workers, and a portrait of Lenin. As he refused to change it, Rockefeller decided to hire another artist to cover it!

58

14852

RADIO CITY MUSIC HALL
6th Avenue and 50th Street, Midtown West, Manhattan

The Rockefeller Center project included a space for the Metropolitan Opera. But it did not come to fruition because of the Great Depression. Radio channels, booming at the time, took his place, which earned the building its name. Radio City Music Hall, inaugurated in December 1932, has a large stage, 44 meters wide and 20 meters deep and the room can welcome up to six thousand spectators. But more than its size, it is its decor that is remarkable. Its designer, Donald Deskey, was hired to completely break with the rococo frills and drapes that had thus far characterized the halls of New York shows. The lobby decor gave more the impression of being in a boat than in a theater. The Art Deco style, simple and austere, was at the height of his glory. Metal, leather, carpet and furniture design composed a chic and refined setting, while giving a sense of wealth and refinement. Giant mirrors, murals, sculptures and modern chandeliers 9 meters high were indeed a contrast with the muses and golden cherubs that audiences were accustomed to. Since 1933, Radio City Music Hall hosts every year at Christmastime the famous Radio City Christmas Spectacular, a popular musical show, performed by famous dancers, the Rockettes.

79627

ST. PATRICK'S CATHEDRAL

5th Avenue, Midtown East, Manhattan

At the end of the eighteenth century, New York's Catholic community was a minority. With Irish immigration and the influx of Catholics a large building was needed. In 1853, the Archbishop launched the idea of building a new cathedral to replace one that was in the south of the city. The Church owned land north of the city, in what was still the countryside. It commissioned James Renwick, a renowned architect, very fond of Gothic Revival. Inspired by the great sanctuaries of Europe, he designed an immense cathedral, in the shape of a Latin cross. The nave, over 100 meters long, and the transept 53 meters long could welcome more than three thousand churchgoers. The two spires stand at over 100 meters high. Tiffany designed two altars. The first stone was laid in 1858, but work, delayed by the civil war, was not completed until 1888 by the addition of spires. In 1920, the writer Francis Scott and Zelda Sayre married at St. Patrick's. The cathedral also held the funerals of Bobby Kennedy, the Senator from New York, after his assassination in 1968. A mass was also called for the death of the artist Andy Warhol in 1987. Although the one of the largest cathedrals in the world, St. Patrick's seems dwarfed by Rockefeller Center facing it and the skyscrapers that surround it.

ST. PATRICK'S CATHEDRAL, NEW YORK CITY 3A-H100

THE ST. REGIS HOTEL
55th Street and 5th Avenue, Midtown East, Manhattan

The wealthy New York families often owed their fortune to successful real estate investments. John Jacob Astor IV was no exception. He had the good idea to build a luxury hotel in Midtown, while the area was booming. The proximity to Central Park and department stores placed it in the perfect neighborhood. In 1901, he launched the construction of St. Regis, an eighteen-story building, in the purest Beaux-Arts style. The first guests were welcomed there in 1904. But the wealthy owner had little time to enjoy the hotel. In 1909 he went on a journey to Egypt and Europe after having scandalized proper New York society by divorcing and remarrying with a lady twenty-nine years younger. On his return in 1912, he had the misfortune of booking a cabin on the Titanic, and died in the sinking. Vincent Astor, the son born from his previous marriage, inherited the hotel, which he sold to a tobacco magnate. In the following years, the St. Regis grew and prospered. The cocktail bar, the King Cole Bar, was one of the favorite meeting points for the chic NYC bourgeoisie. This is where the Bloody Mary was invented in 1934. During the Great Depression, Vincent Astor bought the hotel in 1935 and restored it entirely. He kept it until his death in 1959. The property now belongs to a large international chain of luxury hotels.

The St. Regis Hotel, New York. 96-14

HECKSCHER BUILDING
Madison and 42nd Street, Midtown East, Manhattan

August Heckscher, a German immigrant who made his fortune in coal, iron, and zinc mining, was interested in property development. He was an unusual figure in proper New York society, given his origins. At the beginning of the First World War, he sided with Germany. Some even accused him of using his private yacht for espionage. In 1915, seeking to diversify his investments, he launched the construction of an innovative building. Rather than build a solid block, the architects he had commissioned, Jardine, Hill & Murdock, imagined a tower of twenty-seven floors set back from the street, on a base of a pedestal of five floors. The last few floors are in the shape of a pyramid. This architectural concept, which allowed more sunlight into the street, later entered the urban planning regulations of the city. Completed in 1916, the building contained only medium-sized offices. After the war, Heckscher redeemed himself a proper reputation by becoming one of the largest philanthropists in New York. He created a foundation for disadvantaged or abused children.

Heckscher Building and Belmont Hotel, New York City.

GRAND CENTRAL TERMINAL

42th Street, Midtown East, Manhattan

In the early nineteenth century, the railway arrived in Manhattan. The city was not yet very spread out. But the open track and steam locomotion caused unbearable pollution. In 1871, the owner of the railway, Cornelius Vanderbilt, built a station on 42nd Street. As decrees gradually forced the lines to be buried and electrified, the billionaire had to once again pull out his wallet. The new work involved bulldozed buildings and creating new streets, Madison and Park Avenues, above the buried channels. A new train terminal, more modern and larger, was required to accommodate the influx of travelers and connect to the subway system. It was built between 1903 and 1913. The tycoon called upon the architects Warren and Wetmore. The Beaux-Arts style chosen was that of all the great buildings of the city. A huge amount of granite was used. This stone is naturally radioactive, and it was later realized that the radiation rate is higher than what we tolerate today around a nuclear power plant! On the front, the clock 4 meters high was produce by Tiffany workshops. But it is mostly the inside that amazed travelers. The concourse alone is breathtaking: a ceiling height equivalent to twelve floors, it is painted and electrified to reproduce the heavenly constellations.

Grand Central Depot and Commodore Hotel, New York.

CHRYSLER BUILDING

Lexington Avenue and 42nd Street,
Midtown East, Manhattan

Walter Chrysler had started his career as a railway mechanic. In 1911, he began working for Buick. In 1925, he created his own company and in 1928, he bought Dodge. Two years later, he decided to build his building in New York. This project was supposed to express his passion for the automobile. The architect, William Van Alen, persuaded him to build the highest skyscraper in the world to surpass the Woolworth Building, the record holder at the time. The decoration of the tower provided a great translation of the Art Deco principles. But the originality resided mainly in the steel lining, in the alternation of curves and sharp angles and ornaments recalling the chrome automobile accents. The stylized figure of the eagle, inspired by the car radiator caps, and flickering scales at the top have never been matched. During the construction, which advanced at a rate of four floors per week, the city was full of competitors. Shortly before completion, a rival on Wall Street threatened to be higher. Van Alen then proposed to add a steel coil of more than 58 meters, which was secretly made in four pieces and attached to the building at the last moment, in less than two hours! The record high was reached at 319 meters, including the spire. But the skyscraper was lost its claim as the tallest building less than a year later, to the Empire State Building.

UNITED NATIONS HEADQUARTERS
Midtown East, Manhattan

The decision to install the UN headquarters in New York was taken in London in 1946. To accommodate the new organization of peacekeeping, it was necessary to create an international enclave, which was not easy, given the price of land. Nelson Rockefeller, a member of the project's preparation committee, asked his father, John D. Rockefeller Junior, to pay $ 8.5 million to buy 7 hectares of land occupied by slaughterhouses along the East River and to donate it to the UN. Oscar Niemeyer and Le Corbusier were among the architects who worked on the project. The building had three main buildings. The highest and most visible is the Secretariat Building, a building with thirty-nine floors covered in bluish-gray glass, completed in 1950. It houses the offices of the UN Secretary General. The General Assembly Building, stockier, opened in 1952, hosts the meetings of delegations of the one hundred ninety-three Member States. The last building, near the riverbank, is the Conference Building, where in particular the Security Council meets. With some 5,000 delegates, its 5,000 employees, 2,000 journalists and 2,000 daily visitors, the enclave works like a small, very secure town.

United Nations Headquarters and East River, New York City.

UN3

87261

WALDORF ASTORIA
Park Avenue and 49th Street,
Midtown East, Manhattan

Among the most famous hotels in the world, the Waldorf Astoria is inseparable from the Astor family, one of the most influential in New York. The founders of this prestigious dynasty were butcher's sons originating in Walldorf, Germany. After immigrating to England, one of the Astor brothers, John Jacob, left in 1783 for the United States. He first sold furs, but he soon realized that the key to success was in real estate, which made him the first billionaire in the country. Throughout the nineteenth century, Astor men practically became the «owners» of all Manhattan. Disputes and rivalries were common among senior members of the clan, each wanting to do more or better than the others. Thus, in 1893, William Waldorf Astor tore down his mansion on 5th Avenue to build the Waldorf Hotel. Stung, the wife of his uncle, Caroline Astor, who lived in the adjacent house, did the same in 1897, to build a rival institution, the Astoria Hotel. Luckily his son managed to convince her to move further north, and the conflict eventually worked out. They then connected both hotels, which became the posh Waldorf Astoria. In 1929, the hotel was demolished to make way for the Empire State Building. But it was immediately decided to build a new Waldorf Astoria further north in Midtown, a part of the booming city.

3A-H1291

RITZ TOWER

Park Avenue and 57th Street, Midtown East, Manhattan

Erected in 1925 on Park Avenue, the Ritz Tower appears as a perfect example of the eclectic architecture of New York. The architecture is distinctly Art Deco, with recesses that provide large terraces. The decor is, in turn, inspired by the Italian Renaissance, especially the lower parts made of white limestone. The man behind the project, Arthur Brisbane, was one of the most prominent journalists in the city, the author of columns in major newspapers. At the time of construction, 57th Street had a concentration of luxury boutiques, art galleries and cultural venues such as Carnegie Hall. The Ritz Tower was then the tallest residential building in Manhattan while offering breathtaking city views and a flattering address on business cards. His concept was that of hotel apartments. The suites included living rooms, bedrooms and bathrooms, but did not include a kitchen. A huge central kitchen provided a meal service with relays on each floor. It also had restaurants. This organization offered tenants the amenities of home. Among the prestigious guests of the Ritz Tower, were actresses Greta Garbo and Deborah Kerr and the designer Valentino.

©IRVING UNDERHILL

NEW YORK.

PARK AVENUE
Midtown East, Manhattan

Before the electrification of the railway and the burying of the tracks, Park Avenue was the railway line into Manhattan. The air was unbreathable and the neighborhood, working class. In 1920, it began to have a certain architectural coherence. A succession of important residential buildings was erected, each not exceeding fifteen to twenty floors. This gave a uniform perspective, a bit like two walls flanking the avenue. Park Avenue then became one of the most exclusive addresses in town, and the price per square foot, among the highest in the world. Bordered to the south by Grand Central Station and the MetLife Building (formerly the Panam building), its chic part continues through Midtown East and the Upper East Side to the intersection with 97th Street, where the railway tracks come out of the ground to become aerial. Some of the most beautiful buildings in New York border Park Avenue, such as the Helmsley Building, near Grand Central, the Waldorf Astoria or the Ritz Tower. Before 2010, there was no sign for pedestrians to eleven intersections of Midtown, it was feared that the coverage of railways was too thin to hold their foundations.

3A-H1284

COLUMBUS CIRCLE
AND CENTRAL PARK
Central Park South, Manhattan

Columbus Circle is point zero for measuring distances from New York. It takes its name from the statue of Christopher Columbus, who stands there since 1892. However, it was converted into a roundabout in 1905, to complete the map of Central Park. It's where Frederick Olmsted and Calvert Vaux, the landscape architects of the park, had planned the main entrance. Access to Central Park is guarded by the Merchant's Gate and the USS Maine National Monument, a stone tower topped by a golden sculpture. Before its construction, Central Park was made up of wetlands, where an impoverished population of freed slaves and immigrants without resources lived. In 1853, the municipality bought the land. Work began four years later and lasted twenty years. It consisted in the draining of the swamps, moving huge amounts of earth, dynamite-blasting rocks, creating lakes, planting trees and shrubs... More than twenty thousand workers worked on construction until its completion in 1869. Today, Central Park is essential to life in New York. At the Belle Époque, it was used for the strolls and carriages of the Bourgeoisie. During the Great Depression, it was a temporary haven for thousands of homeless. Later it was the scene of demonstrations against the war in Vietnam and a candlelight vigil after the attacks of September 11, 2001.

COLUMBUS CIRCLE AND CENTRAL PARK, NEW YORK CITY

14795

THE POND
Central Park, Manhattan

When they designed Central Park, Calvert Vaux and Frederick Olmsted wanted to reproduce and preserve a natural and varied space in the heart of the city. It was necessary to provide pathways for walkers, others for horses, others for cars, all without them interfering with each other. It was also necessary to recreate land expanses, waterways and ponds. Of the seven lakes, the largest are the Harlem Meer in the north, the vast Jacqueline Kennedy Onassis Reservoir and The Lake. The most southern one, The Pond, is one of the more surprising because although drowned in vegetation, it offers superb views of neighboring skyscrapers, including the massive silhouette of the famous Plaza. A wide variety of trees and flowers, an artificial waterfall and banks with irregular curves allow a variety of wildlife to settle. A stone bridge is a discreet reminder of human presence. The borders of the Pond have become a birding site, including nearly two hundred species visit the park regularly. Some birds proliferate enormously there: starlings multiplied so quickly that a quarter of all those in North America come from Central Park.

BETHESDA FOUNTAIN
Central Park, Manhattan

The architects of Central Park planned an elegant way central promenade, The Mall, paved, lined with elm trees and dotted with statues of writers. To the north, it leads to a large terrace and stairs down to Bethesda Fountain; a fountain topped the Angel of the Waters. This statue was created in 1868 and inaugurated in 1873 in honor of the Croton Water System, the network that brought Manhattan drinking water since 1842. As a sign of purity, the angel carries a lily in its left hand. The reference was important for New Yorkers, who were victims of terrible epidemics of cholera in the past because of contaminated water. Important detail: the statue was the work of Emma Stebbins, the first woman to be chosen to carry out a public commission in New York. Between the fountain and the upper terrace extended a huge mosaic and a covered porch. The architects wanted the walkers to see and be seen in a stylish location while enjoying the natural beauty of the lake in the background. Today, the terrace and fountain are among the most sought sites for wedding photos, while The Mall is popular with roller bladers and dancers.

BETHESDA FOUNTAIN, CENTRAL PARK

NEW YORK.

PUBLISHED BY L. GOLDSTEIN, NEW YORK.

METROPOLITAN MUSEUM OF ART
Central Park, Manhattan

Wealthy American philanthropists met in Paris in 1866 to celebrate the Independence and had the idea to found a great museum based on the Europe models. The first part of the Metropolitan Museum of Art opened in 1880. The facade of the Beaux Arts style was built in 1902. The museum then never stopped extending until 1990. Most collections come from donations or bequests from private benefactors. All the big names in New York history have left their mark in the form of a room, a wing, a collection or a spectacular purchase. The banker Robert Lehman bequeathed in 1969, for example, three thousand European paintings. These large donations do not prevent the board of directors of the museum, composed of businessmen, lawyers, artists and public figures, to raise funds and conduct an ambitious acquisitions policy. Thus the Met, as it is known familiarly, was the first in the world to buy a painting by Matisse. Today, the museum hosts more than 6.2 million visitors per year.

THE METROPOLITAN MUSEUM OF ART, NEW YORK CITY

27

14821

QUEENSBORO BRIDGE
Upper East Side, Manhattan, and Long Island City, Queens

The Queensboro connects Manhattan to Queens, on the western end of Long Island. The first time its construction was evoked dates back to 1838. However, nothing was done for decades, mainly for financial reasons. When the construction finally began, in 1903, they encountered many problems: endless strikes, sabotage, collapse of a portion of the deck during a storm. The work was not inaugurated until June 1909. Fifty workers were killed during the six years of construction. 1135 meters long, the bridge rests halfway on the small Roosevelt Island, in the middle of the East River. Although totally ignored by tourists, who nevertheless use it to take the subway to the airport, the Queensboro Bridge, with its maze of metal beams painted in beige, is part of the mythical New York. It appears on the poster of the Woody Allen film, Manhattan. For runners of the famous New York marathon, it's the entry point to Manhattan, after crossing Brooklyn and Queens. Since 1976, it can be admired by taking the aerial tramway along its structure, between Manhattan and Roosevelt Island.

QUEENSBORO BRIDGE, EAST RIVER, NEW YORK.

MOUNT SINAI HOSPITAL
East Harlem, Manhattan

In the middle of the nineteenth century, Jews were relatively ostracized. Most hospitals refused to treat them. In 1852, Sampson Simson, one of the first Jewish legal scholars in New York, who obtained his law degree from Columbia University, created a project with eight other philanthropists: the construction of a hospital for their fellow poor. He died two years after the opening of what was dubbed "The Jew's Hospital", on 28th Street. Its religious role was thwarted by the outbreak of the Civil War. The abundance of wounded soldiers and the commitment of Jewish doctors in the fight then changed its profile to become one of the common city hospitals. In 1866 it took on the name of Mount Sinai Hospital. In 1872 it moved to the Upper East Side, where it remains today. A nursing school was established there in 1881. Specialists from Mount Sinai were among the most respected researchers, and some innovations were discovered here, like the first endotracheal anesthesia. In 1968, its medical school was founded. Today, Mount Sinai Hospital is ranked among the best in the world, particularly for heart valve surgery. The list of celebrities who were treated there is long: from the composer Gustav Mahler to the actress Julie Andrews through Harpo Marx of the Marx Brothers, and the dictator Fidel Castro!

Mount Sinai Hospital, New York

AMERICAN MUSEUM
OF NATURAL HISTORY
Central Park West, Upper West Side, Manhattan

The naturalist Albert Bickmore was the spark of the project. He had been a student at Harvard of Louis Agassiz, a zoologist and world famous Swiss biologist. His master inspired him to create the dream of a New York Museum of Natural History. Tirelessly, the young naturalist spoke with politicians and patrons, managing to convince such diverse big names as Theodore Roosevelt Sr., the father of the twenty-sixth president of the United States, or JP Morgan, the philanthropist banker. The creation of the museum was decreed in 1869. Despite limited funds, the first stone was laid in 1874 by the US president himself, Ulysses S. Grant. When the facility opened in 1877, another, President Rutherford Hayes, inaugurated it. Over the years, the building grew. The first building, Victorian style, was completed by an imposing neo-Romanesque part, flanked by turrets. In 1936, it was decided to add a facade of the Beaux Arts style to mark the entrance from Central Park. From 1880 to 1930, the museum financed numerous expeditions and exploration campaigns in the North Pole, Siberia, Mongolia, the Pacific and Africa. It hired renowned researchers, including anthropologist Margaret Mead or paleontologist adventurer Roy Chapman Andrews, who had inspired the character of Indiana Jones.

95

6A-H1599

CATHEDRAL OF
ST. JOHN THE DIVINE
Amsterdam Avenue, Morningside Heights, Manhattan

The imposing St. Patrick's cathedral, the pride of the Catholic Archbishop of New York, taunted the episcopal that dreamed to build something more beautiful and larger. A fundraising campaign was therefore launched in 1887. Four years later, land was bought, and a design competition organized. The successful project proposed an ambitious Roman-Byzantine style that would be a proper response to the Catholic's neo-Gothic rival structure. The plan was to build the largest cathedral in the world, with a nave of 183 meters long! December 27, 1892, the Saint John's Day, the first stone was laid. But problems soon began. It was necessary to dig 22 meters deep to find bedrock, which cost dearly. The first phase of work for the choir and arches holding the central dome took almost twenty years. The death of the first architects also led to a radical change in plans, and it became a Gothic Revival style. The Great Depression did not help the situation, so that the nave was only opened to the public in 1941. Because of the war, manpower and funds were no longer available. Plans were therefore constantly adapted. As a result, the cathedral, consecrated in 1979, multiplies the most diverse styles. Ravaged by fire in 2001, it was reopened after a restoration campaign in 2008.

THE CATHEDRAL OF ST. JOHN THE DIVINE, NEW YORK CITY

4A-H1812

COLUMBIA UNIVERSITY
Broadway and 116th Street, Morningside Heights, Manhattan

The history of this prestigious private university in New York began during the English colonization. Founded in 1754 in lower Manhattan, next to Trinity Church, it was then called King's College. Twenty years after independence, it took the name of Columbia University and moved from Lower Manhattan to Morningside Heights. This is a perfect example of American campus, where academic buildings and dwellings are by side on a single surface of 1.21 square kilometers. Since its inception, Columbia University claims to have counted one hundred and one Nobel Prize among its former students or teachers. It is where the press baron Joseph Pulitzer founded in 1902 the school of journalism, which annually awards the renowned prize that bears his name. Among its buildings, the oldest and most imposing remains the Low Memorial Library, built in 1895 and modeled on the Pantheon in Rome. The interior is full of allusions to mythology, philosophy and Greek and Roman history. Three Presidents studied at Columbia: Theodore Roosevelt, Franklin Roosevelt and Barack Obama. The alumni include celebrities such as billionaire Warren Buffett or the economist Milton Friedman, but also writers Isaac Asimov, J. D. Salinger and Jack Kerouac.

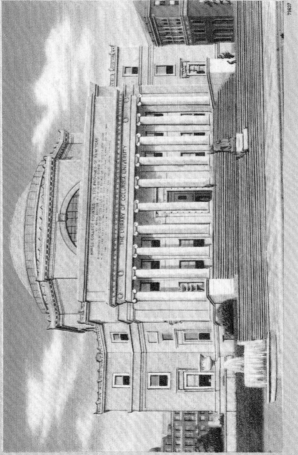

Low Memorial Library, Columbia University, New York City

79637

RIVERSIDE CHURCH
Riverside Drive, Morningside Heights, Manhattan

Riverside Church stands since 1930 along the Hudson. From its conception, this ecumenical church took the Cathedral of Chartres as a model. At its inauguration, it was the tallest church in the United States, topping out with a bell tower 120 meters high. Even the seventy-four bells atop it are grandiose, with their weight of 20 tons, the largest in the world! To consolidate the building, a metal structure was used, making the external buttresses purely decorative. John D. Rockefeller Junior, who financed Rockefeller Center and the MoMA, was behind this project too. A devout Baptist, he wanted to build a church open to all Christian denominations and active on the social front. For the project, he joined Harry Fosdick, a Baptist preacher whose spiritual ecumenist liberalism had pushed far away from the Presbyterian Church. Its positions against racism, segregation and injustice brought him indeed much criticism from fundamentalists. Today, Riverside Church is also a social center. Of the twenty-two floors, ten are vested in classrooms, sports, and theater... More than forty different ethnic communities practice their religion here. Among the groups that meet there, there are associations of gays and lesbians, undocumented workers, and activists against the death penalty.

GEORGE WASHINGTON BRIDGE IN DISTANCE   14828

CITY COLLEGE OF NEW YORK

Convent Avenue, Harlem, Manhattan

The philosophy behind the creation of the Free Academy of the City of New York, in 1847, claimed to offer free higher education to all those who deserve it, regardless of their ethnic or social origin. It was the first of its kind in the United States. It was the idea of Townsend Harris, a businessman who believed in merit. He wanted every talented student and worker to have access to education, even if they were from a freshly arrived immigrant family. The campus he dreamed of mixed rich and poor without prejudice. The Free Academy took the opposite view of the very chic and very elitist Columbia University. This earned him the surname «Harvard of the proletariat.» In 1866, it became the College of the City of New York. However, it was only open to boys. In 1906, the establishment moved into a new campus on a hill overlooking Harlem. It had an imposing neo-Gothic style, inspired by the great English universities. In 1930, a few women were admitted to some degree, but the college only became fully co-ed in 1951. Nine Nobel laureates studied there, the most recent being John O'Keefe, the laureate in medicine in 2014.

CITY COLLEGE OF NEW YORK, NEW YORK CITY.

14796

BROOKLYN BOROUGH HALL
Downtown, Brooklyn

Brooklyn's history dates back to the first Dutch settlement in the seventeenth century. Its rural profile changed in the early nineteenth century, with the opening of a first shipyard. The establishment of a regular line of ferries in 1814 resulted in more affluent families coming to live while retaining their activities in Manhattan. In 1834, when the community was erected as an independent municipality, there were thirty thousand inhabitants, of all ethnic and religious backgrounds. Two families of large landowners, Pierreponts and Remsems, who had worked for the independence of the city, then donated land for a town hall, City Hall, for which was laid the foundation stone in 1836. But money was scarce; it was stuck at the foundation-level. Work resumed in 1845, with a neo-classical architecture, and was completed in 1848. Fifty years later, Brooklyn was incorporated into New York to become one of the five boroughs. City Hall then became the Borough Hall. It was nearly destroyed in the 1930's on the grounds that it could no longer fulfill the functions for which it was designed, but no project of substitution prevailed, and in 1966 the building was listed a landmark. It now stands at the edge between the area of Brooklyn Heights, including beautiful sandstone houses that line the East River and Downtown Brooklyn, the administrative center.

Borough Hall, Brooklyn, N. Y.

203

73946

BROOKLYN BOTANIC GARDEN
Prospect Park, Brooklyn

In 1859, Brooklyn was the third city in the United States, behind Manhattan and Philadelphia. Convinced that a vast park would enhance the attractiveness of their city, its elected officials, led by James Stranahan, appealed that year to the designers of Central Park, Frederick Olmsted and Calvert Vaux. The so named Mount Prospect Park was to include a museum, the Brooklyn Museum. A botanical garden, the Brooklyn Botanic Garden, was also part of the final project. It extended over 16 hectares and was opened in 1911. Harold Caparn its landscaper began with a garden based on the wild local flora, to which he added several themed gardens, over the next thirty years. In 1914, the Children's Garden opened, the first in the world to be integrated into a botanical garden. Children could cultivate a plot like in community gardens. In 1915, a pond and its banks were a turned into Japanese garden by a landscaper from Tokyo. In 1941, one of the most beautiful attractions of the garden, its collection of Japanese cherry trees, was planted. It colors a plaza in pink when flowering. Among the buildings that dot the garden, administrative buildings, built between 1912 and 1917 and covered in tiles in a Tuscan fashion, were listed landmarks in 2007. As for conservatory greenhouses dating from the same era, they contain collections of bonsai and rare orchids.

201:— BOTANICAL GARDEN, PROSPECT PARK, BROOKLYN, N. Y.

CONEY ISLAND
Brooklyn

One of New York beaches is located south of Brooklyn, on the coast of this former island that was gradually joined to the mainland by silting of the channel. The first European settlers came to hunt rabbits (coney is a popular equivalent of "rabbit") but it hardly had any interest for city dwellers, until the fashion of sea bathing made it the perfect recreational escapade. In the second half of the nineteenth century a bathhouse building and seafood bars began to attract an ever-growing crowd. The proliferation of shacks led the city to regulate the development of the small resort. In the early twentieth century, a wooden promenade was built to skirt the sandy beach, 4 kilometers long, and ensure access. The northern promenade was reserved for entertainment. The first, launched in 1901, was called «Trip to the Moon», a kind of ship that carried visitors to space. The following year, the project to build an amusement park was born. It opened as Luna Park in 1903. In the 1920's, the first Ferris wheel, «Wonder Wheel» was built. In 1927 it was the arrival of the roller coaster, called «Cyclone». 1957 Coney Island welcomed the New York Aquarium. In 2012, Hurricane Sandy ravaged Coney Island, but the entertainment reopened the following year.

452.—PARACHUTE JUMP, BEACH AND BOARDWALK, CONEY ISLAND, N. Y.

48440

BRIGHTON BEACH
Brooklyn

Brighton Beach extends Coney Island's boardwalk. It too is located on the southern shore of Long Island. But the comparison stops there because Brighton Beach seems to belong to another planet. The beach is not lined with fry shacks or rides, but Russian and Jewish restaurants where you can appreciate the perogies and borscht while drinking vodka. The area is nicknamed «Little Odessa» for the large number of Jewish immigrants of Russian origin who settled there after World War II. This is also the New York area that matters most to Holocaust survivors. Russian is the language that you'll hear the most, and signs and menus are usually written in the Cyrillic alphabet. After the collapse of the Soviet Union, new immigrants were added to the first Jewish wave, definitively fixing the Eastern European identity of places. Schools, administrations, banks and even a Russian-speaking theater make up the neighborhood. In the shadow of parks, grandfathers in cap play backgammon while babushkas stroll between the stalls of sour cabbage and smoked fish. As for the beach itself, it now hosts Ukrainian, Georgian and Uzbek emigrants.

SCENE AT THE STONE WALL, BRIGHTON BEACH, N. Y.

FLUSHING MEADOWS-CORONA PARK
Flushing, Queens

Known worldwide thanks to the US Open, Flushing neighborhood extends to the center of Queens, between LaGuardia and JFK airports. During the time of Dutch and English settlements it was an agricultural area. With the explosion of immigration in the nineteenth century, the village took on a cosmopolitan character, with more than 50% of Asians. However, it remained surrounded by vast unexploited areas for quite a while. When New York prepared to host the World's Fair of 1939, this was the site that was chosen. The so named Flushing Meadow Park occupied an area of almost 500 hectares. The World's Fair's goals were overtly commercial: to promote the revival of business and profit, after ten years of economic depression. Most stands boasted advances in science, color photography, air conditioning, nylon, the electric typewriter and 3D movies. The public even saw an appearance of Superman! More than 44 million people came to visit. From 1946 to 1951, some of the buildings temporarily hosted the UN before its Manhattan headquarters was completed. Another World's Fair was held at Flushing Meadows in 1964, during which the park was renamed Flushing Meadows-Corona Park.

8A-H947

New York World's Fair 1939

HELL GATE BRIDGE
Wards Island, Manhattan and Astoria, Queens

During the American Revolution, Randalls and Wards Islands, served as the bases for English armies that wanted to attack Manhattan. In the mid-nineteenth century, they were assigned to the establishment of social institutions: orphanages, a center for young offenders, rest homes for veterans and a cemetery for the poor. Then they became specialized in the care of poor immigrants, before becoming home to the municipal asylum. In 1899, with four thousand four hundred patients, they housed the largest psychiatric hospital in the world. In 1916, the islands were opened up thanks to the construction of a double bridge, the Hell Gate Bridge. Joining the Queens, the bridge initially spanned a strait of the East River called Hell Gate, hence its name. Then it connected the islands to Bronx crossing the Bronx Kill, a channel of the Harlem River. The metal structure was considered the most robust of all those bridges of the city. Initially, the bridge was to be made of a system of metal girders, but some feared that residents of the asylum could climb to escape. So they opted for tours made of smooth masonry. Today, the bridge is restricted to railway tracks, and it is owned by Amtrak. The channel between the two islands was filled in early 1960.

HELL GATE BRIDGE, NEW YORK CITY

ROCKAWAY BEACH

Hammels, Queens

At the southern part of Queens, Rockaway Beach borders a narrow peninsula of Long Island that two villages shared. In the nineteenth century, one of the big landowners in the area, Louis Hammel, decided to develop the site, and donated land to open a railway and a railway station. In 1897, the combined hamlets became Rockaway Beach, which was incorporated the following year, with Queens, in New York City. The arrival of the train and urban development quickly made the town a popular resort. An amusement park opened in 1901. But getting to the beach was still difficult, as you had to work your way around Jamaica Bay to enter the peninsula. The construction of two bridges in 1937 and 1939, improved access. The first linked the west end to the south of Brooklyn. The second allowed access to the center of Queens. Rockaway Beach then evolved into residential suburbs, especially since the subway soon replaced the train. Buildings along the coast transformed the landscape into an urban beach. Since the early 2000s, the place has come into fashion, attracting skateboarders, surfers, hip-hop fans and artists. The vegan or Latino canteens have multiplied between the bars and espresso counters cupcakes. In 2012, Hurricane Sandy almost wiped out Rockaway, carrying houses, the boards of the boardwalk and some of the sand from the beach.

Surf Bathing, Rockaway Beach, L. I., New York

R-1

BRONX PARK

Bronx

Jonas Bronck was the first to settle in this area in the seventeenth century. This former captain played a big role in the peace treaties with Indians. His lands were sold over time, and in 1890 the New York Park Association acquired a part in creating a park. The following year, more than 100 hectares were vested in the New York Botanical Society, and the same area was allocated to the New York Zoological Society in 1898. The new Bronx Park also included large areas of lawns, groves, recreation areas and sports fields. The design of the botanical garden rested, meanwhile, in the tireless commitment of Nathaniel and Elizabeth Britton. These botanists had met at Torrey Botanical Club, the oldest American botany club. Their common passion for plants led them to visit the Royal Botanic Gardens of Kew, in London, during their honeymoon. That's when they had the idea to create a similar one in New York. Upon their return, Elizabeth launched into frantic lobbying to raise money, without status or compensation. Her efforts were rewarded, but it was her husband, a professor at Columbia University, who was named director of the Botanical Garden. Elizabeth remained a volunteer throughout her life. Despite her many respected publications, she never received a position at the university.

BOAT HOUSE, BRONX PARK, NEW YORK CITY.

YANKEE STADIUM
South Bronx, Bronx

The most famous baseball team in America, based in Baltimore, moved to New York in 1903. During its history, it counted legendary players like Babe Ruth or Joe DiMaggio. The latter was also known for having married Marilyn Monroe. But it was the former who allowed the rise of the Yankees. George Ruth, aka The Babe, is now considered the greatest baseball player of all time. He joined the Yankees in 1919 and marked a turning point for the team, who then played at the Polo Grounds, a Harlem stadium owned by the rival team the Giants. Thanks to him, the Yankees surpassed their opponents, and became loved by New Yorkers. Stung, the leaders of the Polo Grounds then begged them to build their own stadium, as far as possible from them…but the Yankees chose the Bronx across the Harlem River, less than 2 kilometers from the Giants. Their new stadium consisted of three rows of balconies surrounding the entire field and offering fifty-eight thousand seats. The Babe and his throws and hits brought the spectators. The success was such that it is nicknamed the stadium «The House That Ruth built». When the player died in 1948, his body was exposed at the entrance. Over ten thousand fans came to pay tribute. The stadium has since received the most diverse events, Pink Floyd and U2 concerts and masses during Papal visits.

THE YANKEE STADIUM, NEW YORK CITY.

MORRIS HIGH SCHOOL
South Bronx, Bronx

Morris High School was the first high school in the Bronx. Its foundation in 1897 was within the framework of education reform, set up by the City of New York. At that time, the proliferation of bad neighborhoods concerned social services, especially as the growing number of immigrants organized themselves into ethnic or religious communities. The intolerance of the first migrants, mainly Anglo-Saxon and white, rendered the assimilation of new immigrants difficult. Meanwhile, the rich were aware of new ideas, especially in terms of child psychology and educational methods. Their goal was to solve integration problems through education, in a paternalistic manner and with a Protestant rigor. To keep control of these new populations, they thought it was necessary to centralize the organization of teaching. Morris High School in the Bronx fills exactly this role, integrating waves of immigration of Jews from Central Europe, blacks, Puerto Ricans and Hispanics. Its success has never wavered, since throughout the twentieth century, it has produced students of undeniable success, such as the Nobel Prize in Medicine Hermann J. Muller (1890-1967), filmmaker Jules Dassin (1911- 2008), or the Secretary of State Colin Powell (born in 1937).

Morris High School, 166th street and Boston Road, Bronx, New York.

PORT RICHMOND
Staten Island

The first settlers, of Dutch and French origin, arrived in Port Richmond in the late seventeenth century. They built a church and cemetery, around which the village grew. The biggest landowners, the Haughwouts, Dutch immigrant descendants, became the heads of the small community. In the 1830's, they inspired the geometric plan of the city, similarly to the street-grid in Manhattan. It was then a bustling city that used the port to transport the vibrant local industry's products: wood, coal or production of linseed oil. In the nineteenth century, among local celebrities born near Port Richmond, was the wealthy Cornelius Vanderbilt (1794-1877), who made his fortune in railroads and ferries to Manhattan. Port Richmond was connected at that time to New Jersey by a ferry service, which was interrupted after the completion of the Bayonne Bridge in 1931. The construction of the Verrazano-Narrows Bridge in 1964, which connects Staten Island to Brooklyn, signaled the decline of the small city. Economic activity then moved on the east coast of the island. Later, major black and Mexican immigration gave rise to racial tensions, exacerbated in 2014, when an African American was killed during his arrest.

8:—Richmond Ave. Port Richmond, Staten Island, N. Y.

TO LEARN MORE

Arthus-Bertrand (Yann), Tauranac (John), *New York, une histoire d'architecture,* La Martinière, 2002.

Barelly (Christine), *New York,* coll. « Grands Voyageurs », Le Chêne, 2013.

Berenholtz (Richard), Johnson (Amanda), Willis (Carol), Giroldi (Cécile), *Architecture de New York,* Flammarion, 2004.

Charyn (Jerome), *New York : chronique d'une ville sauvage,* Gallimard, 1994.

Cohen (Jean-Louis), *New York,* Citadelles et Mazenod, 2008.

Cohen-Solal (Annie), Goldberger (Paul), Gottlieb (Robert), *New York 1945-1965, art, vie et culture,* Hazan, 2014.

Collectif, *Comprendre New York,* Larousse, 2015.

Couture (Charlélie), *New York by CharlElie,* Le Chêne, 2009.

Weil (François), *Histoire de New York,* Fayard, 2005.

The Little Book of Paris

by Dominique Foufelle
ISBN : 978-2-81231-331-8

IN THE SAME COLLECTION IN FRENCH

Le petit livre des explorateurs,

Le petit livre des expériences,

Le petit livre de la vie de Jésus,

Le petit livre des dieux,

Le petit livre des lieux chrétiens,

Le petit livre de Noël,

Le petit livre des rois de France,

Le petit livre de Louis XIV,

Le petit livre de la Révolution,

Le petit livre de Napoléon,

Le petit livre des grands personnages,

Le petit livre des citations historiques,

Le petit livre des grandes dates de l'histoire,

Le petit livre des départements,

Le petit livre de la Bretagne,

Le petit livre de Paris,

Le petit livre de la Tour Eiffel,

Le petit livre des villes et blasons,
Le petit livre des châteaux,
Le petit livre des châteaux de la Loire,
Le petit livre de la France gourmande,
Le petit livre des métiers d'autrefois,
Le petit livre des expressions familières,
Le petit livre des Fables de la Fontaine,
Le petit livre des symboles,
Le petit livre des jeux d'enfants,
Le petit livre des bébés,
Le petit livre de l'école,
Le petit livre des chats,
Le petit livre des chiens,
Le petit livre des arbres,
Le petit livre des fleurs,
Le petit livre des champignons,
Le petit livre des plantes médicinales.

All the images in the book are from the private collection of
Éditions du Chêne.

Cover: Background : © Coll. privee MA/Kharbine TA ;
Front cover © Éditions du Chêne.

© 2016, Editions du Chêne - Hachette Livre for the English edition
© 2016, Editions du Chêne - Hachette Livre for the original edition

Editorial Director: Flavie Gaidon
with the collaboration of Franck Friès
Editor: Sandrine Rosenberg
Artistic Director: Elodie Palumbo
Under the direction of Sabine Houplain
Proofreader: Myriam Blanc
Layout and photogravure: CGI
Translation © Editions du Chêne – Hachette Livre, 2016
Translation by James Geist
English layout: Emilie Serralta
Sales and partnerships: Mathilde Barrois
mbarrois@hachette-livre.fr
Press Relations: Hélène Maurice
hmaurice@hachette-livre.fr

Published by Éditions du Chêne
(58 rue Jean Bleuzen, CS 70007, 92178 Vanves Cedex)
Printed in China by Guangzhou Hengyuan Printing in July 2017
Copyright Registration: September 2016
ISBN 978-2-81231-532-9
24/8462/5-02